T0197383

Lil' Hal's

Giant Christmas Box

Christy B

Illustrated by Rumar Yongco

AuthorHouse™
1663 Liberty Drive
Bloomington, IN 47403
www.authorhouse.com
Phone: 1 (800) 839-8640

Because of the dynamic nature of the Internet, any web addresses or
links contained in this book may have changed since publication and
may no longer be valid. The views expressed in this work are solely those
of the author and do not necessarily reflect the views of the publisher,
and the publisher hereby disclaims any responsibility for them.

Any people depicted in stock imagery provided by Getty Images are models,
and such images are being used for illustrative purposes only.
Certain stock imagery © Getty Images.

This book is printed on acid-free paper.

ISBN: 978-1-7283-3251-2 (sc)
ISBN: 978-1-7283-3252-9 (e)

Library of Congress Control Number: 2019917407

Print information available on the last page.

Published by AuthorHouse 10/28/2019

authorHOUSE®

It was Christmas morning. Lil' Hal could hardly get his legs to go into his pants as he dressed to see what is under the Christmas tree. After an additional struggle with uncooperative shoes, he is thump! Thump! Thumping from step to step. He flew into the living room, and his mouth flew wide open.

"Where are all the presents?" he shouts louder than he expected.

It surprised his mother so much she ran from the kitchen asking harshly, "What is all the noise about?"

Near tears, Hal pleads, "Where are all the presents?" then adds, "Was I bad?"

"No! No!" his mom coos, as hugging his shaking body.

Lil' Hal feels the tears running down his face. He is sure he had never been this disappointed. His mom wipes away the tears with a corner of her apron and hugs him tighter.

"I'll explain when your dad comes down for breakfast. By the way, grandpa and grandma are coming, too," she assures him adding, "Patience is a gift bigger than you can expect."

"Do I smell homemade waffles and sausage?"

"Hal, you have a very good nose," his mom confirms. The two go into the kitchen to finish breakfast preparations. Just then his grandparents quietly slip in the front door to spread gifts under the tree. Having finished that task, they seat themselves at the dining table, which is now full of breakfast food.

Hal forced his legs to hold still, carefully chewing the last sweet morsels of waffles and sausage.

"Now! to the tree!" grandpa announces, and everyone went to a seat in the living room.

"What is all this?" Lil' Hal asks, staring at a pile of presents, "Wow!"

Hal's dad says, "You may pass out the gifts one by one."

"Okay!" He feels his chest swell with the honor of his important job.

Slowly the packages are passed out until only one very giant box remains.

"Whose present is this? I can't see a name tag!" shouts Hal, while his dad scoops him up to help him see the name on top.

"It says Hal," he screams.

"Go for it, kiddo!" everyone shouts.

Ripping paper sounds fill the room as paper flies all over the floor. Then again and again like Russian-nesting dolls, until there are eight boxes on the floor. At the center is one very small box, certainly the awaited prize of potential greatness. Everyone else has found wonderful gifts but. . . Pouty lips form as he stares at a note, from the bottom of the box. It reads, "Look for the red stocking on the tree."

Hal grabs the red stocking, which seems empty. A tear rolls down his cheek as a big sniffing sound is heard. Frustrated, he squeezes the stocking, which feels crinkly. He now knows there is a paper with a string attached. Another message, "Use me to wind up the string that is tied to your gift."

Skipping in circles Hal begins winding the string then he moves upstairs. Bedroom to bedroom he is lead to the closet upward to the attic. The growing ball of string leads him to his basement then out the back door to his grandparent's basement. Continuing to wind string, Lil' Hal moves through the maze of rooms in his grandparent's house. Upstairs and downstairs until every room is entered then out the front door through his grandfather's store.

Now, outdoors he shivers in the snowy cold without a coat following the stringy trail. The growing ball is basketball-sized, still, there is no present. His hot, angry cheeks are keeping him warm thinking, "Could this be one of his dad's super big practical-jokes?"

Hal stomps through the snow. A vision of his family laughing and taking photos of him fills his mind. "Hal the fool!" It didn't help when he hears a giggle emitting from the garage. He thinks, "They can't fool me" . . . "I won't be surprised" . . . He grabs the door handle, throwing the door wide open and braces himself for a camera flash.

But he is, very, very surprised because there is more than the family with cameras . . . There is the most beautiful go-cart he had ever seen or dreamed. His head spun. Lil' Hal knows how much he is loved by his family. Thank you's, kisses, and hugs go round the garage for everyone. " What a very Merry Christmas indeed!!!! Patience did give me more than I expected!"

Printed in the United States
By Bookmasters